CHRISTIAN POEMS.

CHRISTIAN POEMS.

BY THE

REV. TIMOTHY HARLEY.

"Let the word of Christ dwell in you richly in all wisdom; teaching and admonishing one another in psalms and hymns and spiritual songs, singing with grace in your hearts to the Lord."—*Colossians*, III., 16.

Second Edition. Revised and Enlarged.

LONDON: PRINTED FOR THE AUTHOR.

1867.

LONDON: YATES AND ALEXANDER, PRINTERS,
CHURCH PASSAGE, CHANCERY LANE.

TO THE RIGHT HON.

THE EARL OF SHAFTESBURY, K.G.

My Lord,—

Having received permission to lay this little work at your Lordship's feet, in doing so I cannot refrain from expressing my deep sense of the privilege conferred upon me in being suffered to inscribe your honoured name upon so mean a page. The Lord greatly reward all those acts of exemplary kindness and goodwill for which your Lordship is universally characterised; and, when you have finished your useful course on earth, may your Earldom be exchanged for a Kingdom,—your coronet of gold for a Crown of Glory that fadeth not away.

This book is a handful of spiritual seeds, which have been steeped in earnest prayer, and which are now scattered broadcast, with humble trust that they may produce a rich harvest to the glory of God. The sling is hurled by a feeble hand; may heaven direct the stones: the bow is drawn at a venture; may the arrows pierce many a heart. And if these Poems, in the hands of the Divine Spirit, shall be made manna to the hungry soul, wine to the heavy heart, water of life to the thirsty spirit, or light to any that walk in darkness, my warmest and highest wishes will be granted.

Consecrating this work to His praise "whose I am and whom I serve," and craving for it your Lordship's indulgence and favour,

I have the honour to subscribe myself,

My Lord,

Your Lordship's obedient servant,

TIMOTHY HARLEY.

CONTENTS.

CHRISTIAN POEMS.

"TO DIE IS GAIN."

Phil. i. 21.

I SHALL one day sleep the sleep of death;
I shall one day breathe my latest breath;
And the soul that now is bound in clay,
Will the fetters break, and fly away.

Then the voice that now is heard below,
Singing pilgrims' songs as home I go,
Will be lost to those on earth I love,
To be found engaged in hymns above.

Then the ear that now delights to gain
From the Gospel's news the ease of pain,
With surprising rapture will rejoice
At the welcome sound of Jesus' voice.

Then the eye that now is dimmed with grief,
Or lit up with hope of near relief,
Will for ever close on things terrene,
To re-open where my God is seen.

I shall then behold my Saviour's face,
And survey the traits of matchless grace;
While the wounds received on Calvary
Will recall to mind the cursed tree.

To be like my Lord,—with Him to dwell,—
To be safe from Satan, sin, and hell,—
Are the joys to which my heart aspires,—
Are the only heaven my soul desires.

Shall I sigh or tremble when I think
That I soon shall reach the river's brink,
When I know that Jesus will be near
To support my faith, to soothe my fear?

For as Israel walked o'er Jordan's bed,
And the waters at their presence fled,
So the waves of death's oft-dreaded tide
To make room for me will all divide.

Then the Lord, who guides and guards my way
In a fire by night, in cloud by day,
Will not leave me till secure I stand
On the shores of rest—the promised land.

Then with speedy steps I'll homeward press,
As a pilgrim through this wilderness;
And no thoughts of death my heart shall pain,—
While "to live is Christ, to die is gain."

LINES READ AT A HARVEST HOME MEETING.

DEAR Christian friends! we greet you,
Right glad are we to meet you
In this social way;
We come, our joy expressing,
And wish you every blessing
On this happy day.

Thou who dost send the harvest:
To Thee who never starvest
Either man or beast,—
To Thee let loud thanksgiving
From every creature living
Sound from west to east.

With holy jubilation
Our vows of adoration
Heartily we pay;
Lord! own the praise we render,
And hear the prayers we tender
On this happy day.

We pray for you, dear people,
That, though no gaudy steeple
Crowns this sacred place,
You may possess the tower,
Which God's almighty power
Builds on sovereign grace.

Oh! may our Lord and Master
Emit upon your pastor
Many a cheering ray;
God comfort and defend him,
Prosperity attend him
From this happy day.

May you that are his deacons,—
While in the world as beacons,
Set to warn and guide,—
In nothing damp or pain him,
But constantly sustain him,
Standing by his side.

While one in Church communion,
May Christian love and union
Never here decay;
May God each member nourish,
And make your church to flourish
From this happy day.

May many find salvation,
Among the congregation
In this house of prayer;
May many hearts be broken,
As God's most blessed token,
That His love you share.

And when we meet in glory,
You'll tell a joyful story,
How God did display
His grace, in far exceeding
The gifts for which we're pleading,
On this happy day.

"I WILL COME AGAIN."

THE WORDS OF THE LORD JESUS.

Let not your heart be troubled: ye believe in God, believe also in me. In my Father's house are many mansions: if it were not so, I would have told you. I go to prepare a place for you. And if I go and prepare a place for you, I WILL COME AGAIN, and receive you unto myself; that where I am, there ye may be also. I will not leave you comfortless: I will come to you. The world seeth me no more; but ye see me: because I live, ye shall live also. My peace I give unto you: not as the world giveth, give I unto you. Let not your heart be troubled, neither let it be afraid. Verily, verily, I say uuto you, That ye shall weep and lament, but the world shall rejoice: and ye shall be sorrowful, but your sorrow shall be turned into joy. Ye now have sorrow: but I will see you again, and your heart shall rejoice, and your joy no man taketh from you. Till then I will never, no never, no never leave you, nor forsake you; for lo! I am with you alway, even unto the end of the world. These things I have spoken unto you, that in me ye might have peace. In the world ye shall have tribulation: but be of good cheer: I have overcome the world.

HE WHICH TESTIFIETH THESE THINGS SAITH,

SURELY I COME QUICKLY.

A LITTLE while ago the glorious Spring,
With countless charms, inspired the Poet's strain;
But soon for other climes it spread its wing,
And left us, singing, "I will come again."

We heard the cuckoo sound the glad return
Of vernal joys; but now we hark in vain;
For while his note makes other ears to burn,
We've but his echo, "I will come again."

We walked our Father's garden with delight,
And saw such beauties as can entertain
The greatest minds; now that enchanting sight
Is past, but in a trice will come again.

The violet, the lily of the vale,
The primrose, snowdrop—where are they? we fain
Would cull them, and their rich perfume inhale;
But no, we cannot till they come again.

We stood one eve and watched the summer's sun,
Sinking mid golden sky and silver main;
He shortly his diurnal race had run,
Leaving the promise, "I will come again."

Sweet picture of the man whose spirit flies
To rest in Jesus, and with Him to reign;
Before he leaves his earthly friends he cries,
"Weep not for me, ye'll see my face again."

For though the ransomed Christian bids adieu
To scenes of earth, for him to die is gain;
Though he departs, 'tis but to live anew
In Heav'n, whence he shall never come again.

One night, when all was clear, we saw the moon
  Gliding in close attendance on his train
By whom she shines; but she her crescent soon
  Concealed, while whispering, "I will come again."

Like her we travel through this sphere terrene,
  Approaching more the Sun the more we wane;
Anon we cry, and hide beneath His sheen,
  "The hour is near when I will come again."

How often we've been called to bid farewell
  To those united by affection's chain;
And as we've pressed the lips we loved so well,
  We joyed, remembering we should meet again.

Had he but known the kiss would be the last,
  Oh! who shall tell our agony and pain?
But, as a final look our fond eye cast,
  We felt persuaded we should meet again.

So those disciples, gathered round their Lord
  Before His death, could scarce from grief refrain;
When in the wound the kind Physician poured
  This healing balsam—"I will come again."

"Let not your hearts be troubled, ye believe
  "In God, He ever will your Friend remain;
"One who will ne'er be faithless or deceive—
  "With Him I leave you till I come again.

" In His eternal house not made with hands
  " Are many mansions ; there ye shall obtain
" A portion with me on my throne, which stands
  " For ever—wait till I shall come again.

" Why are you sad because I go away ?
  " 'Tis to prepare a place for you ; refrain
" From mourning, speedily will dawn the day
  " When in my glory I will come again.

" You've followed me through ills of every kind ;
  " Through toil, and trouble, misery, and pain ;
" Forsaking all your all in me to find ;
  " And I'll reward you when I come again."

What tender words ! who but the Lord of love,
  With matchless kindness filling every vein,
Could comfort thus ? and now He reigns above,
  We've still the sentence, " I will come again."

We oft lament because the time appears
  So very long ; our murmuring hearts complain,
And moaning cry, " Nearly two thousand years
  He's tarried ; will He ever come again ?"

Whenever our impatient spirits rise,
  And thus repine, we'll instantly restrain
Their passion, and remind them He's more wise,
  And better knows the time to come again.

Poor Jonah was displeased exceedingly
When Nineveh her pardon did obtain;
And we shall deal as selfishly as he,
If peevish till the Master come again.

The Lord's not slack, as some men slackness count;
Two thousand years with Him are but a grain,
Though to our eyes they seem an Alpine mount;
'Tis but a moment ere He'll come again.

The reason why His chariot wheel delays,
Is not because He ceases to retain
A fond remembrance of those mournful days
When first He promised "I will come again:"

He rather waits because His matchless love
Holds in His wrath, and gives His grace the rein;
Over the deluged earth He sent His Dove,
And now is slow to call it home again.

Instead of sorrowing, let us each go forth
To labour and endure with heart and main:
Till angels raise the cry from south to north,
"Virgins, arise! your Bridegroom comes again."

'Tis but a little while ere yonder sky,
As did the Temple's vail, shall cleave in twain;
Those wide ethereal gates shall open fly,
To let the King of Glory come again.

He'll come, not as the Babe of Bethlehem,
Born to be mocked, and treated with disdain;
E'en those who once delighted to contemn,
Will own His power when He comes again.

At first He had no form nor comeliness,
And those who looked for beauty looked in vain;
But every tongue shall speak His loveliness
When wreathed with rainbows He shall come again.

His eye, once red with weeping, shall be bright
With lustre that shall make the day-star wane;
His brow, once crowned with thorns inwove with spite,
Shall gleam with garlands when He comes again.

When first He came, the Heir of poverty,
He had no resting-place through earth's domain;
But now He tenants vast Infinity,
And as the Lord of all will come again.

Oh happy day! fell Satan then shall cease
To vex our souls, and be our constant bane;
For where no tempter can disturb our peace
We shall be borne when Jesus comes again.

How often here below we heave a sigh
Because we fail perfection to attain;
But with this cheering truth our eyes we dry—
I shall be like Him when He comes again.

The world, a scene of vanity and noise,
No longer shall our heaven-fixed minds detain;
Gladly we'll part with all its guileful toys
When He, to whom they're nought, shall come again.

Our spirits here have had no other nest
Than our frail bodies, feeble, and inane;
And to afford them everlasting rest
Their gracious Lover soon will come again.

Transporting day! we'll watch its hastening dawn,
And spend the fleeting moments that remain
Preparing for the resurrection morn,
When our unsetting Sun shall rise again.

Our chief desire shall be to imitate
Our great Example, who was free from stain,
That we in constant readiness may wait,
However long, till Jesus comes again.

Nor will we hang our harps on willow boughs,
Our happy spirits shall rejoice amain;
Why should despondency o'ercloud our brows
If our Deliverer shall come again?

Disconsolate old Jacob sorely grieved
Because he thought his favourite son was slain;
He cried with anguish, "Me have ye bereaved;
Joseph is gone, and ne'er will come again."

Ah! yes, he will, poor Israel, be not sad,
  Thy gracious God has chosen to ordain
That Joseph should be Egypt's lord; the lad
  Still lives; thou shalt behold his face again.

When Jacob saw the wagons near his door,
  The cheering sight o'ercame his aged brain;
He soon revived, and said, "I need no more;
  "Before I die I'll see my child again."

"These things are all against me," is *our* groan,
  While heavy griefs oppress; till we regain
Our hope, and cry, "My Lord, whom I bemoan,
  Is yet alive, and soon will come again."

That broken-hearted mother of the dead
  Had trod with lighter steps the streets of Nain,
Had he, for whom she mourned, when dying, said,
  "Weep not, dear mother, I shall come again."

Mary and Martha long before had dried
  Their sorrows for their brother who had lain
For brief repose in death, had he but cried
  "Jesus will shortly call me back again."

And we shall turn to spangles many a tear,
  Like as the sun turns drops of dew or rain,
By recollecting that the Lord is near,
  And as our life will quickly come again.

Poor Magdalene stood weeping at the tomb,
  Because its cave did not her Lord contain;
But oh! how swiftly she forgot her gloom
  When Jesus said, "Mary, I've come again."

Often we mourn that all within is vile
  And all without is wickedness profane;
But hark! One speaks above, "A little while,
  And to convey you home I'll come again."

Therefore, instead of sighing let us sing,
  Be joy, not grief, the burden of our strain;
We'll burst the fetter, mount the golden wing,
  And fly to meet Him as He comes again.

He comes! He comes with clouds to try the world;
  Before His bar all nations to arraign:
Now shall His foemen be to ruin hurled,
  For as the vengeful God He comes again.

He comes! and every eye shall see His face;
  And they that slew their Friend, more cruel than Cain,
Shall reap a full reward for that disgrace
  They cast on Him:—As Judge He comes again.

He comes to cause a universal change,
  To turn the hills and valleys to a plain;
To open many things we now count strange,
  And shall, till He—our Prophet, comes again.

The problem—why the rich man rolled in wealth,
While Lazarus was poor—He'll then explain;
Why saints are sick, while sinners sport in health,
He will interpret when He comes again.

The Christian's now, like Joseph, in the cell;
Our Pharaoh comes that he with Him may reign:
He's now, like Daniel, in the den; to quell
The furious foe our Helper comes again.

He comes! behold His harbinger appears;
Millions arise to life from land and main:
To check the motion of a thousand spheres,
To close the scene of time He comes again.

Come Jesus, come! we'll hail triumphantly
The glad event; our longings will attain
Their zenith when our eyes Thy face shall see:
Amen! come quickly; Jesus, come again!

SONNET TO THE SUN.

ROLL on! thou golden globe of glory, roll!
 In dazzling brilliancy pursue thy course:
 And may thy swift obedience strike with force
On every passion of my sluggish soul.

Fly on! stupendous orb of splendour, fly!
 Though, since thou first didst spread thy wings of light,
 Thou hast not rested on thy glorious flight,
Still, strong as ever, thou dost gild the sky.

Speed on! resplendent ball of brightness, speed!
 For soon thy glittering journey will be o'er;
 When Jesus comes, thou'lt be required no more,—
His lovely face thy beams will supersede.

Press on, then, blazing Sun, with ardor press!
And usher in the Sun of Righteousness.

"BEWARE OF DOGS."

Beware of dogs that lick
With flattery's poisonous tongue;
Such only wait your bones to pick
When the bow of life's unstrung.

Beware of dogs that fawn
And cringe about your feet;
A noble mind such brutes will scorn,
And with indignation treat.

Beware of dogs that bark,
And think to terrify;
Let them alone, and every spark
Of their harmless fire will die.

Beware of dogs that growl
At nothing or a feast;
These cynic curs must snarl and scowl,
'Tis the nature of the beast.

Beware of dogs that whine
In tones of howling grief;
'Tis casting pearls to worthless swine,
To bestow on such relief.

Beware of dogs that bite;
And guard against the hound
That seeks in blood its chief delight,
For it everywhere is found.

Beware! when wealth comes in,
In comes your canine friend;
When fortune smiles dog-days begin,
In adversity they end.

Then all avoid these dogs,
Which do by far more harm
Than savage hogs, or blazing logs,
Or London fogs, or Irish bogs,
I'd almost said, than dangerous grogs,
Which have with some no charm.
So bear the watchman's loud alarm,
Let us all beware of dogs!

CHRISTIAN SYMPATHY *v.* CRUEL SLAVERY.

Ye sons of Britain brave!
Commiserate the slave,
That, far across the sea,
Is groaning to be free:
His prayer to heaven ascends;
Jehovah's ear attends;
And soon the freedman's cry
Shall round the circle fly,
While every hill and dale
Re-echoes on the gale
The shout of liberty,
The slave! The slave is free!

Ye who abominate,
And will not tolerate
With least impunity,
Accursed tyranny;
Espouse their cause who fly
Before the fiendish eye,

Or wail beneath the slash
Inflicted by the lash
Of those inhuman brutes
Which Satan here deputes
To execute his laws,
And aid his murderous cause.

People of God, awake!
Your honour is at stake,
As representatives
Of him who ever lives
Captives to liberate.
I charge you advocate
Their claims whose moans arise,
Whose blood, like Abel's, lies,
And calls aloud on heaven
That vengeance may be given.
Stewards of God, awake!
You must the fetters break.

Stay not for senators,
Or their executors:
Look not to kings and queens;
Trust not in ways or means:
What are societies?
Or their auxiliaries?

All are a feeble clan,
Vain is the help of man.
If we should wait for them
Ere we the current stem,
When would the tyrant flee?
When would the slave be free?

Oh ye who know the Lord!
Arise with one accord,
And use your influence
With God's omnipotence:
'Tis not by dint of arms,
Or cruel war's alarms
The conquest will be won;
If e'er the work be done
The Lord must interfere:
Emancipation's near
If Christians bend the knee,
And cry, "The slave set free!"

Did not the Master say
"Whatever when ye pray,
Ye ask ye shall receive?"
If we this word believe,
Oh let us intercede,
And for our brethren plead;

And, as the Lord exists,
Before the morrow's mists
Shall cool the early breeze,
The suppliant on his knees,
Shall hear the answering word
"In heaven thy prayer is heard."

O God! our souls inspire
With more intense desire
To see the hour appear
When far abroad and near
All shall be wholly free.
It fills our hearts with glee
To know that many a slave
Has proved that power to save
Which thou art never slack
To shew to white or black:
But now we want to see
The slave *from man* set free.

And when, throughout the world,
Thy potent arm has hurled
Grim slavery back to hell,
With its arch-founder fell:
Then still thy chariot ride;
Sinners from sin divide;

Charge all from south and north
"Prisoners of guilt! come forth."
Say of the sons of woe,
"Loose them, and let them go!"
Till, universally,
All shall be doubly free.

"LOOK UP."

Psalm 5. 3.

A SAILOR boy high up the mast,
 Looked downward from the giddy height,
And growing dizzy as he cast
 His eyes on deck, was filled with fright;
The captain cried, "All danger's past,
 If to the top you turn your sight;
 Look up!"

So as we scale the steeps which lead
 To heav'n, "the city on a hill,"
How oft these accents thence proceed,
 And with delight our spirits fill,
 "Look up!"

This motto cheered the Israelites,
 As through the waste they took their way;
In darkened days, in darker nights,
 The cloud and pillar seemed to say,
 "Look up!"

The leaves of truth the lesson teach
  That help in God alone is found:
The Gospel we rejoice to preach,
  Is vocal with the joyful sound,
            "Look up!"

Sinner! dost thou desire to find
  Redemption for thy captive soul,
Or balm to heal thy wounded mind?
  Then on the Lord thy burden roll,
            "Look up!"

Christian! by Satan sorely tried,
  Do vile temptations vex thy heart:
Thou hast His sympathy whose side
  Was piercéd with every deadly dart,
            "Look up!"

Poor saint! who hast each morn to cry,
  "Give me this day my daily bread;"
To him direct thy downcast eye,
  Who had not where to lay His head;
            "Look up!"

Afflicted saint! thy pain is great,
  The billows toss thy feeble bark;
But soon the waters shall abate,
  And thou shalt rest thy weary ark;
            "Look up!"

Bereaved believer! has thy loss
  Crushed all thy joy? there's One above
Who'll help thee bear thy heavy cross,
  And fill the vacuum with His love;
    "Look up!"

Devoted saint! with zeal toil on,
  Thou soon shalt lay thy sickle down:
Soldier! the victory now is won,
  And shortly thou shalt wear the crown;
    "Look up!"

Aged believer! to the last,
  On Jesus' arm for succour lean;
Whene'er thy sky is overcast
  Raise thy dim eyes from things terrene,—
    "Look up!"

Dying believer! on life's brink,
  About to navigate the sea
Of endless bliss, should nature shrink
  In death, the last extremity,—
    "Look up!"

"WAR IN HEAVEN."

Revelation xii. 7—9.

There was a time—we grieve to know 'tis past,
And sometimes fear it never will return—
When perfect Peace her smile o'er nature cast,
And made its youthful heart with bliss to burn.

Our world was then in infancy; the eye
Of man, its living soul, was always bright;
His face was like a summer's cloudless sky,
His heart was ever glowing with delight.

Sin had not yet employed the plough of care,
So on his placid brow no furrow dwelt;
The bending load of sorrow and despair,
His upright frame as yet had never felt.

'Twas just before these halcyon days began,
That God from deepest solitude arose:
Long had He cherished thoughts of love to man,
Which thoughts He now determined to disclose.

His sovereign will became the corner stone,
  On which He built the universal pile;
He founded first his everlasting throne,
  Then laid the scene of time's momentous trial.

The work fulfilled, His arm the ruling rod,
  O'er vast creation's boundless empire swayed;
All—all was governed by the hand of God,
  Whose mighty mandate everything had made.

Co-partner of His throne there sat a queen,
  Equal in power, majesty, and grace,
Her God-like form was clothed with dazzling sheen,
  And beauty found perfection in her face.

Like her eternal consort she was formed
  Of uncreated essence, and possessed
Life self-existent, quenchless, and informed
  With all to make her reign supremely blessed.

Peace was the Queen that ruled the universe,
  Angels and man were subjects of her realm:
Each tongue was fired her glories to rehearse,
  Each bosom loyalty did overwhelm.

The sceptre of her wide dominion waved
  Across the range of each revolving star;
Ten million worlds her gentle guidance saved
  From crumbling in one dread tremendous jar.

(If peace and order left the rolling spheres,
  Oh what disastrous havoc would be made!
Instead of standing fast six thousand years,
  Globe after globe would be in ruins laid.)

While she the banner of her love unfurled,
  All hearts acknowledged her supremacy;
Such golden days as shone o'er every world
  Beneath her sway, some never more shall see.

Ah, never! though the Prince of Peace again
  Shall come to end the din of strife below,
Yet, in the land of everlasting pain,
  None shall the blessing of her presence know.

We say her royal jurisdiction spread
  O'er everything her potent Lord had made;
The countless legions of the sky she led,
  And all her laws were everywhere obeyed.

But soon a dire catastrophe occurred,
  Which threatened to dethrone this glorious queen
It, like a hurricane, those waters stirred,
  Which erst were as a sea of glass serene.

The how and whereby are a mystery,
  But cruel envy reached some heavenly mind,
Wrote the first page of ruin's history,
  And laid the plot to overturn mankind.

The dread Supreme sat on His lawful throne,
  And spotless Adam walked the new-made earth,
While the conspirator retired alone
  To fix his plans and give his project birth.

To banish from his seat the mighty God,—
  To hold himself the reins of government,—
To make his fellows bow to kiss his rod,
  And own him monarch,—were his foul intent.

But when he thought of God's omnipotence,
  And of the legions He to arms could call,
He charged himself with vilest arrogance,
  And well nigh let his scheme entirely fall.

However, as the possibility
  Of gaining others to revolt arose,
He kindled with fresh hopes of victory,
  And hushed his fear of failure to repose.

While base ambition heated every vein,
  And burning thirst for glory marred his breast,
He little dreamt of that undying pain,
  Which at this moment gnaws his wretched breast.

He re-assembled all his scattered powers,
  And bade his courage stand immovable;
Then, fearing lest in heaven's ambrosial bowers
  He should be missed, he left his citadel.

He soon was lost amid the countless throng
  That glistened in the sweet perennial smile
Which lit the lips of Peace, and turned to song
  The tongues of all, save his—made dumb by guile.

This plotter sang not; his malicious eye
  Was rivetted on her, who sat enthroned
Amid resounding anthems loud and high,—
  While from his heart her sceptre he disowned.

Sin is a weed that will not long remain
  Beneath the ground, it must spring forth and grow;
Like leaven in the meal, it spreads amain;
  Like ocean's streams, its nature is to flow.

One day we cast a pebble in the wave,
  And when the cause was lost, the effect we proved;
With rippling wreath on wreath it hung its grave,
  Till all the surface of the flood was moved.

Such was the progress of that wickedness
  Which turned to silence heaven's harmonious lays;
It rapidly increased, till perfect bliss
  Melted like wax before the furnace blaze.

A host of rebels eagerly conspired,
  And with the traitor sought their Sovereign's fall:
The leader cried, " Of servitude I'm tired,
  Henceforth I'll reign the potentate of all.

By the allegiance you to me have sworn,
I charge you summon all your martial powers,
Heroic minds, to noblest triumphs born!
Convince the Foe that heaven's throne is ours."

While these impassioned words, like arrows fly,
Prolonged reverberations meet his ear;
So livid lightning darts athwart the sky,
And leads the rattling thunder in the rear.

They pledged themselves his orders to attend,
And he protested they should share the spoil;
How that momentous tragedy would end,
Alas! they thought not midst their dread turmoil.

The traitor his embattled army led,
And towards the seat of power they made their way:
The Queen, sweet Peace, at their advancing fled
To where in halcyon harbour Adam lay.

But God, the mighty God, unmoved remained,
And eyed the rebels as they gathered round;
With words imperious they His name profaned,
With haughty mien they on His honour frowned.

Oh, what a scene! could not the Lord have said,
"Spirits! is this your kindness to your Friend?
Do you, but streams from me the Fountain-head,
Assail the life on which your lives depend?"

What rash conceit! what impious arrogance!
  When creatures which possess no other might,
Than what they borrow from Omnipotence
  Lift up their puny hands with God to fight.

Almighty God! and didst Thou move an arm,
  When weaklings such as these assailed thy power?
Did their devices fill Thee with alarm,
  Or force Thy flight to some sequestered bower?

Nay, nay! as when at first creation rose
  In swift obedience on Thy dread demand;
So in the utter downfall of Thy foes,
  They flew like chaff before Thy fierce command.

When the forked courser shoots along the storm,
  The rumbling wheels of thunder's chariot troll;
Then sylvan oaks, of huge gigantic form,
  Like corn before the sickle prostrate roll.

So as those pompous spirits God defied,
  A vivid flash of anger left His eye;
Anon His awful voice, with thunderings cried,
  " Depart, ye cursed, from my presence fly."

Profoundest terror with the sentence fell,
  And those thus doomed would fain their acts recall:
But see! from heights of bliss unspeakable,
  Vast legions of defeated angels fall.

Glory to God! he spake, and all was done;
He drove the rebels down to deepest woe:
He rose upon them, like the mid-day sun,
And they, before His heat, dissolved like snow.

Like shooting stars they fell from bliss untold—
Like withered leaves they dropped from glory's tree;
While in their track eternal sorrow rolled,
Like a huge avalanche of misery.

Hail! Mighty Victor, none shall take Thy throne,
Though millions more rise up the work to try:
The kingdoms of creation are Thine own,
And they shall rue the day who Thee defy!

Ye faithful Cherubim and Seraphim!
We wonder not that you astonished stand,
And fear to look upon the face of Him,
Whose awful frown no power can withstand,

But be not troubled, tune anew the lyre,
And make the triumph of your God your song;
He kindled for his foes his righteous ire,
And endless shouts of praise to Him belong.

He on their heads has poured the latest vial
Of deathless wrath, and barred Heaven's massive
See! He returns, and wears His natural smile, [door:
The cloud He but assumed is seen no more.

Go forth to meet Him, lay your honours down
  Before His feet, and magnify His might:
With Hallelujahs weave a wreath to crown
  The dreadful Champion coming from the fight.

He comes, and with him brings His glorious queen,
  Whose heavenly reign will be disturbed no more;
The Lord has fixed a bridgeless gulf between
  Those Spirits which began the woeful war.

So far from Heaven is their dark domain,
  That if they would, they never could return;
Their sun has set, and ne'er shall rise again,
  Their lamps are out, and never more shall burn.

To mount again His firm unshaken throne
  Jehovah comes; Angels! your music bring;
With loftiest pæns His dominion own,
  Cry, "Reign for ever, universal King!"

THINKING OF JESUS.

Jesus! chief star of Heaven's pole
Fixed centre of my roving soul,
Round whom its thoughts as planets roll,
Help me to think of Thee.

My heart is like a wayward sheep,
Which will not near its Shepherd keep;
Oh! make it o'er its follies weep,
And draw its thoughts to Thee.

It wanders here and there to find
Some new enjoyment to the mind,
And leaves its best delight behind—
Failing to think of Thee.

The broken cistern, Lord, destroy,
And bring me to the fount of joy,
Whence pleasures flow without alloy,
That I may think of Thee.

Draw off my eyes from earth and sin,
From all without and all within,
And let not worldly care nor din
Disturb my thoughts of Thee.

With Mary I will take my seat,
Beneath thy face, before thy feet;
Oh! make my meditation sweet,
While there I think of Thee!

Thou always wast, as now Thou art,
In the affection of Thy heart;
My spirit ever shared a part—
Thou long hast thought of me.

Before the angelssang their birth,
Or Adam lived in heaven on earth,
E'en in eternity thy girth
Of thoughts encircled me.

When on the cross Thy sacred brow,
Smarting with thorns, was seen to bow,
It bent, as oft it bendeth now,
With thoughts of love to me.

Thou did'st forsake the ark above,
And o'er the world, like Noah's dove,
Did'st fly to show thy saving love
To sinners like to me.

Then back to Heaven Thou soon did'st go,
To lead the way from guilt and woe;
And in the midst of triumph's glow
Thou still did'st think of me.

Why Thou with love to me should'st burn,
Before I breathed, I cannot learn;
I could not love thee in return,
I could not think of Thee.

And since the hour when I was born,
I've oft requited thee with scorn,
And yet I'm on thy bosom borne—
Yet Thou dost think of me.

Ah! I remember well the days,
When in my own destructive ways
I walked regardless of Thy praise,
And never thought of Thee!

Poor foolish child! I loved my play,
And rather chose to go astray
Than on Thy arm my head to lay,
And sweetly think of Thee.

It grieves my heart to know that I
Thus passed Thy matchless mercy by,
Nor ever stopped to heave one sigh,
Nor spend one thought on Thee!

Was this my kindness to my Friend?
Why did'st Thou not, O Jesus, send
My soul to pains that never end,
To make it think of Thee.

Thy grace, dear Saviour, was too strong,
Thy love was kind, and suffered long;
Thou therefore did'st my life prolong
Till I should think of Thee.

But that, my Lord, had never been,
Had'st Thou not come to intervene,
And stand my sins and me between,
To draw my thoughts to Thee.

One look on Thee convinced my mind
That I before was doubly blind,
Or why did I no pleasure find
Whene'er I thought of Thee.

The peerless beauties of Thy face,
The richness of Thy matchless grace,
As shown to our degenerate race,
Were thoughts averse to me.

But when Thy touch unsealed my eyes,
My soul was fill'd with glad surprise,
Such charms I then could recognise,
'Twas heaven to think of Thee.

But ah! a host of guilty fears
Soon pierced my breast like poisoned spears;
My cheeks were overflowed with tears,—
I could not think of Thee.

Like clouds that hide the noon-day sun,
So rose the evils I had done;
In vain I tried the sight to shun,
In vain to think of Thee.

Then written on the frowning sky,
That awful sentence met my eye,
"The soul that sinneth it shall die:"
Oh! whither shall I flee?

"I quake while Sinai's thunders roll,
And lightnings flash from pole to pole,
Great God! take pity on the soul
Which fain would cease to be.

Enclosed with fires of wrath I stand,
Stretch out, O God, thy potent hand,
And pluck me as a flaming brand
From hopeless misery.

From self, the world, and sin, I run,
My only hope is in Thy Son,
A rebel, ruined, and undone,
I cast myself on Thee."

Cried Justice stern, " God has decreed
Whoever breaks His laws shall bleed,
Then how, vile soul, can'st thou be freed?
There is no hope for thee."

" Oh must I perish? must I die?
To no dear refuge may I fly?
Must I in endless torments lie?
For ever woe is me."

Then bitterest tears my speech did choke,
O'erwhelm'd with grief no more I spoke,
My heart in deepest anguish broke,
All hope seem'd fled from me.

But though my sorrow was so great
While in that deep despairing state,
Yet, to be saved 'twas not too late,—
There still was hope for me.

What though the darkness yield no beam,
Joy cometh with the morning's gleam,
And though my case did desperate seem,
There was a hope for me.

For while I stripped and wounded lay,
And wished in vain to see the day,
A Gracious Friend passed by that way,
Who turned to look on me.

And as He gazed, His lovely face,
Shone like the sun, while full of grace,
His eyes beheld my woeful case,
And wept with love to me.

The glorious change His presence wrought
Was great beyond all human thought;
Then, in a voice with kindness fraught,
He spake in love to me.

"Poor soul! compassion fills my breast,
While I behold thee thus distressed,
And till I set thy heart at rest,
I will not go from thee.

But I will save thee from thy foes,
And set thee free from all thy woes,
If thou wilt in my power repose,
And trust thy all to me.

Dost thou renounce thy former ways?
Wilt thou devote thy future days
To living to thy Saviour's praise?
Wilt thou believe in me?"

"Ah, Lord! Thou art a Friend indeed,
Thou visitest me in my need;
And though I am a bruised reed,
Thou still dost notice me!

I am a helpless child of man,
Condemned by God's most righteous ban,
Which ever since my life began
Has hovered o'er me.

As such, with nought to recommend
My ruined soul, O precious Friend!
Before Thy feet I humbly bend,
And give myself to thee."

He gently took me by the hand,
And softly whispered, " Sinner, stand!
I'll lead thee from this dreary land,
If thou wilt follow me.

I'll take thee from this world below
To fields where greenest pastures grow,
And living waters gently flow,
If thou wilt follow me.

But e'er we seek that happy sphere,
I've many things to show thee here,
Such as thy downcast heart will cheer,
Come, sinner, follow me."

As we pursued our pleasant way,
And as began the dawn of day,
My joy increased, I could but say,
" 'Tis good to follow Thee."

He answered, "As thou seest the night
Vanish before the shining light,
Which shineth every hour more bright,
So shall it be with thee.

Thy sins and griefs shall disappear,
Thy sun each moment shine more clear,
Till, as in heaven thou dost appear,
Thy day shall perfect be."

And first to Bethlehem we came,
"The house of bread" (expressive name),
Where Christ, the Bread of Life, became
A little child for me.

He told me of His wondrous birth,
And how He came to live on earth
To ransom souls of priceless worth
From endless misery.

And then He said, "Before we trace
My course through life, a little space
We'll turn aside, and view the place
Where I was slain for thee.

Poor sinner! raise thy tearful eye
To yonder sacred spot, where I
Did once in bitterest anguish die
To purchase life for thee."

I looked to see the hallowed site,
My bosom glowing with delight,
When like a vision of the night
My Jesus fled from me.

Oh! how shall I describe the smart,
Which, like a dagger, pierced my heart,
When called so soon from Him to part
Who had been heaven to me.

His being absent from my view
A curtain o'er my spirit drew,
A dark eclipse my comfort knew,
For He was heaven to me.

But as I mourned my bitter loss,
The sackcloth which had hung across
My thoughts removed, and lo! a cross
My weeping eyes did see.

And on that cross there hung a man
Whose face was worn, whose cheeks were wan,—
Down which the trickling tear-drops ran—
Whose eyes were fixed on me.

Thus He my fluttering heart addressed,
"Poor soul! with sin and sorrow pressed,
Would'st thou with life and joy be blessed?
Then fix thy thoughts on me.

Dost thou not know me who I am?
I am Jehovah's paschal Lamb,
Required to die, like Abram's ram,
That Isaac may go free.

My hands are bound to break the chains,
My side is pierced to ease the pains,
My blood is shed to cleanse the stains
Of wretched souls like thee.

The law of God I've magnified,
Its claims I've fully satisfied,
That whosoe'er in Adam died
May live again in me.

And now if thou can'st but believe,
Pardon and peace thou shalt receive,
And at this cross thy burden leave;
Dear sinner, trust in me."

I answered, "Though of sinners chief,
I do believe, and with the thief
Who on this spot found sweet relief,
Cry, 'Lord, remember me."

He then exclaimed, "Father, forgive
This trembling soul, and bid him live;
Unloose his iron bands, and give
His spirit liberty."

No sooner had the Saviour ceased,
Than every fetter was released;
My joy so rapidly increased,
I seemed in heaven to be.

The *gate* of heaven it must have been,
For suddenly in dazzling sheen,
The angel of the Lord was seen
Close to that cross and me.

He took away my filthy dress,
Removed each trace of leprousness,
And with a robe of righteousness
Completely covered me.

Then said the angel "Go in peace,
In every heavenly grace increase,
And when thy earthly course must cease,
I'll come again to thee."

Anon he spread his wings of light,
And like a sunbeam took his flight,
Leaving my cup of pure delight
Brimming with ecstacy.

But though he vanished from my view,
One still remained whom well I knew;
I nearer to his presence drew,
And He drew near to me.

The cross was gone, and not a trace
Of sorrow lingered on the place,
Yet I remembered well the face
Which sweetly smiled on me.

'Twas He who first had turned aside
To view my low estate; who dried
My gushing tears, and mollified
The wounds which covered me.

'Twas He whom on the cross I saw
Bedewed in sacrificial gore;
Whose blood could cleanse whoe'er should draw
Near to that sacred tree.

'Twas *Jesus*, who, with beaming eyes,
Beheld my rapturous surprise,
Which, like the light when more doth rise,
Was new-born joy to me.

Jesus! I love this retrospect;
And when my devious mind is wrecked
On rocks of doubt, thus to reflect
Bears it renewed to sea.

Should other recollections stray,
Yet to the hour of death shall stay
My fond remembrance of the day
When first I thought of Thee.

For though my passions then were strong,
Such as to young recruits belong,
Yet oft the subject of my song
Has since been sweet to me.

For when cast down with sin or care,
Or well nigh driven to despair,
I've found relief in humble prayer,
In thinking, Lord, of Thee.

Too oft each wordly mount I've scaled,
To every port my bark has sailed,
And when each earthly source has failed,
I've turned at last to Thee.

Would that I first Thy face had sought,
For every disappointment taught
My foolish mind that earth yields nought
But empty vanity.

So still, whene'er my heart is pained,
The Balm of Gilead is obtained,
And health and comfort are regained,
By thinking, Lord, of Thee.

When Satan tempts me to rebel,
Or strives to drag me down to hell,
I only can his force repel
By thinking, Lord, of Thee.

Whene'er I need a faithful guide,
To lead me up the mountain's side,
Where numerous graves are gaping wide,
Jesus, I think of Thee.

Or when I need a pilot's hand,
To steer my vessel to the land,
Through seas which mightiest ships could strand,
Jesus, I think of Thee.

Whene'er my spirit would repine,
I weigh Thy crushing griefs with mine ;
Was ever sorrow like to Thine?
Thine was fierce agony.

If by discouragement I'm grieved,
And cry, " Who hath my words received?"
At once I'm solaced and relieved
By thinking, Lord, of Thee.

Men would not hear Thee in Thy day,
And if from me they turn away,
It is because they hate Thy way,
And will not think of Thee.

Yet should they Thee or me defame,
May I unflinchingly proclaim
The saving virtue of Thy name,
And live to honour Thee.

And if my life on earth be spent
In imitating Thee, who went
About with every power bent
To bless humanity.

Then when Thy soul is satisfied
By witnessing Thy perfect bride,
I, with the hosts of glorified,
Shall share Thy joy with Thee.

Then shall Thy servants see and know,
That every seed they sowed below
Was registered by God, although
They sowed it weepingly.

Till then enable me to preach
To whomsoe'er my voice can reach,
And when the work is done, may each
Result be left to Thee.

Whether my earthly pilgrimage
Be closed in youth or hoary age,
May I each hour my thoughts engage
In thinking, Lord, of Thee.

To hymn Thy glories never tires
Angelic harps or saintly lyres,
Though without interlude the wires
Are swept to honour Thee.

As a reflector of their lays,
May I converge my borrowed rays
In the same central theme of praise,
In magnifying Thee.

And when my work on earth is done,
The battle fought, the victory won,
When the short race of life is run,
In death I'll think of Thee.

I'll turn to those who gave me birth,
To some of even greater worth,
But the last thought conceived on earth,
Jesus! shall dwell on Thee.

When on the edge of life I stand,
I'll, at Thy call, my wings expand,
And, turning from the weeping band,
Will wend my way to Thee.

Leaving the stars beneath my feet,
I'll rest not till I reach Thy seat,
And there my joy shall be complete
In thinking, Lord, of Thee.

Made free from sin, of grief devoid,
By no distracting care annoyed,
Eternity shall be employed
In thinking, Lord, of Thee.

THOUGHTS ON SPRING.

Hark to the little birds which sweetly sing;
How gladly they announce the birth of Spring.
Preserved through chilling wind, and frost, and snow,
These choristers their gratitude would show.
And while their music captivates my ears,
Awake! my heart, and join these chanticleers.
While sunny smiles on earth's old furrowed face,
Of winter's frowning aspect, take the place;
While from its annual sleep, mid cold and gloom,
Our hemisphere wakes up, afresh to bloom;
While all is jubilant with joyful praise,
Arise! my soul, to God an anthem raise.
Almighty Father, who of old did'st plan
And form this world a dwelling-place for man:
Where'er I look—adown—around—above—
Thy wisdom shines in characters of love.
In all my eyes behold Thyself I trace:
The sun reflects the brightness of Thy face;
The cloudless sky bespeaks Thee free from stain;
Thy paths are pictured on the watery main.

On every page of nature's tome I find
Some holy lesson bringing Thee to mind.
Alas! our hearts are so depraved by sin,
So full of earth, God seldom enters in.
Though man alone has reason to discern
Creation's charms,—alone a heart to yearn
With love to Him by whom that structure came,—
Alone a soul in which the sacred flame
Of admiration dwells,—yet often he
Is last and least in nature's psalmody:
Though of all creatures most from him is due,
His hymns of praise are far between and few.
Great Architect of yon blue vaulted dome,
Spread like a curtain round our earthly home;
Who hast the earth with verdant grass arrayed,
Beneath our feet, like a green carpet, laid;
Who from creation's anvil struck the sun,
And sent that blazing ball through space to run;
Who spake, and all things out of nothing came
To trumpet forth the glory of Thy name;
O send a seraph with a living coal
To touch my mouth, to set on fire my soul,
That, while I contemplate this scene most grand,
My lips may tend to magnify Thy hand.
Of Thy great works I know not how to speak,
In lauding Thee my strongest notes are weak;
Yet, deign approvingly to hear my lays,

Till found in heaven I yield Thee nobler praise.
Thou Son of God! o'er all for ever bless'd,
Who on Thy works Thine image hast impressed:
Each glorious object that my eye beholds
Some of Thy beauties to my mind unfolds.
Whate'er I view suggests the pleasing hint,
Thy book of metaphors is still in print.
For when the earth was honoured by Thy feet,
When Thou did'st breathe its air so mild and sweet,
From nature Thou did'st cull Thy similies
To form foundations for Thy homilies.
The blue expanse of ether o'er my head,—
The bright refulgence from our centre shed,—
The spreading trees, whose leaves and shady boughs,
God's band of feathered songsters nurse and house,—
The birds themselves, whose mellow, warbling throats,
Pour forth the sweetest, most enchanting notes,—
The gold and silver gem-besprinkled mead,—
The sheep that on its pastures lie and feed,—
The ploughman's share upturning yonder soil,
His eye stretched forward, lest his work should spoil,—
The broad high road by which so many pass,—
The strait, but pleasant way, o'ergrown with grass,—
All bring to mind Thy words of truth and grace—
Leaves from the tree of life to heal our race.
While I this scene survey, my spirit soars,
And, passing through the everlasting doors,

Stands in the presence of the great *I AM*,
And sings the song of Moses and the Lamb.
While this transporting scene delights my eye,
My soul on adoration's wings would fly.
Thou Word of God, by which the heavens were made,-
To whom the morning stars their homage paid,—
Who left Thy dwelling in the realms of bliss
To sojourn in a blighted world like this,—
(For though 'twas stainless when its course began,
'Tis sadly altered through the fall of man ;)
Whose advent here below the angels sang,—
At whose return the bells of glory rang,—
Who now in yonder better land dost reign,—
Who soon in pomp wilt visit earth again,—
Who art Thy Father's and Thy people's joy,—
Whose glories all the harps of heaven employ,—
O drop a sparkle of celestial fire
Into my breast, and my dull tongue inspire,
That while I muse the fire within may burn,
And I the way to praise Thee more may learn.
Instruct me how I best may spread Thy fame,
And to my fellow men Thy love proclaim.

And Thou, Eternal Spirit! just and good,
Who o'er the waters dark of old did'st brood;
Who, like a dove, did'st sit upon His head,
Who, through immersion's wave, his followers led,—
Thou who at Pentecost did'st prove Thy might

By bringing thousands into Gospel light,—
Who still dost plant within the sons of earth
The new existence of the second birth,—
As on this exhibition grand I muse,
As nature's bulky volume I peruse,
I read, in diction forcible and clear,
The words, " The Spirit of the Lord is here."
The muse again is on her airy wings,
Again the honour of her God she sings :—
Almighty Regent of the Prince of Peace,
Whose blood-redeemed dominions still increase;
Invisible Baptizer with the fire
Of love divine, which makes the soul aspire
And pant for pleasures never found below,
Pleasures which only new-born spirits know;
Thou secret Wind, whose source and destiny
Are to our shallow minds a mystery;
Thou gently falling Dew; thou cooling Rain;
Thou mollifying Oil, easing the pain
Of sinners wounded by the two-edged sword
Of the convincing terrors of the Lord;
Thou precious Paraclete to all that mourn;
Thou Consolation of the soul forlorn;
Oh ! for a bosom full of heavenly love,
That while I think on Thee, Thou tender Dove,
My heart may overflow with praise divine,
And all that praise, blest Spirit, may be Thine.

Eternal Father! Son! and Holy Ghost!
From whom sprang forth the universal host
Of angels, who are still preserved from sin,—
Of devils, who Thy grace shall never win,—
Of men, designed to show Thy glory forth
Either in endless bliss or endless wrath,—
Of suns,—of moons,—of stars,—with all that lie
Beyond the compass of the human eye;—
Thou self-existent, unseen Trinity,
Whose habitation is infinity,
Thinking of Thee my spirit doth amaze,
O how can I a worthy anthem raise!
Great God! how mean, how vain my praises seem
When once contrasted with their mighty theme.
O for a voice louder than loudest thunder,
To cleave the everlasting hills asunder,
To make the oceans heave, the mountains flame,
Yea, all the earth to shout its Founder's fame.
Glory to Him who built the spangled arch,
And sent its shining legions on their march:
Glory to Him who formed this earthly ball,
And all upon it, whether great or small.
Glory to Him who, when He trod this world,
His people's enemies to ruin hurled.
Glory to Him who doth from sin release,
And guide our vessels to the port of peace.
Be this the chorus of creation's host,—

Glory to Father, Son, and Holy Ghost!
  Hark to the plumaged tribe! how sweet their song!
Unweariedly their music they prolong.
Of praising God these warblers never tire,
Nor rest they till in silence they expire.
But, while my ear is ravished with the birds,
My mind is in a maze in seeking words
To represent the splendour of the scene
Of earth re-animated, gay, and green,
But where can words be found that shall express
The peerless charms of nature's vernal dress?
There are no words; God's works are so sublime
They ne'er were spoken by the tongue of time.
Though every syllable were big with thought,
Man's narrow language here falls very short.
Our best conceptions too are far behind,
Our feeble faculties are so confined;
And sooner could we grasp the rolling sun,
Than we could understand what God has done.
Before this task the greatest mind would bend;
All may admire, but none can comprehend.
God's works, like God Himself, are so profound,
No human plummet can the bottom sound.
Then how can I, with my rude pen, essay
A tribute equal to the theme to pay.
O how shall my untutored pencil limn
A picture worthy of the works of Him

Whose beauty decks the earth in colours bright,
Whose pure effulgence floods the world with light?
This Gabriel could not do: I only seek
To sketch His work, that I His praise may speak.
While I pourtray, kind Spirit, suffer not
My sin-stained pen Thy handiwork to blot.
(The painting, like the painter, is so grand,
'Tis always marred if touched by human hand.)
Instead of raising mists to hide Thy face,
Aid me to make Thee clearer, God of grace;
May all my meditations yield Thee praise,
Till earth's are hushed in heaven's purer lays.
 Relying on the guidance of that Friend,
Who to the searching soul His help will lend,
I would the beauties of the scene explore,
Which as I view it charms me more and more.
The new edition of the Book of Spring
Before me lies; in it are songs to sing,—
Lessons to learn,—rare wonders to admire,—
Fuel with which to light a sacred fire
Of exultation,—themes for Christian joy,—
Pleasures that satisfy but never cloy,—
Reasons for lowliness of life and heart,—
Matters for prayer,—and God in every part.
The Book of Nature's like the Book of Grace,
A mirror to reflect its Author's face.
Each page presents these words in speech most grand,

Here is thy Father's and my Writer's hand.
  How changed doth Nature's countenance appear!
Only as yesterday 'twas dull and drear.
I saw it then in darksome habit clad,
And paused to think what made it look so sad;
Till I considered of the year that's gone,
And fancied earth had put its sackcloth on
To mourn the death of eighteen-sixty-three,
So lately buried in eternity.
But now that dismal Winter's far away,
And Spring hath shown his face so blithe and gay,
We seem to live in quite another world,
Where fresh delights are every day unfurled.
The blooming alterations we behold,
Make all look young again, which erst looked old.
Each object seems from torpitude to be
Emerging into new vitality.
The verdant vesture of the whole display
Differs from Winter's as doth night from day:
And earth for clothing now (the flowers note)
Like Joseph, has a many-coloured coat.
But while I o'er these transformations range,
The question rises, what has caused the change?
Has He who paints the grassy blade with green,—
Who fills with scent the violet unseen,—
To whom the birds ring out their melting songs,—
To whom the praise of vernant joys belongs,—

Has He transmuted and become more bright?
Has He received, and therefore gives, more light?
True, His imperial orders sway the spheres,
But is He altered by the altering years?
Nay, verily! Jehovah is the same;
"I never change" is his peculiar claim.
Vicissitude may stamp Creation's brow,
God ever was, and will be, e'en as now.
Though Nature's turning wheel be mutable,
The Pivot ever is immovable.
Whence then doth youthful spring derive its birth?
And what effects the seasons of the earth?
Is it not yonder golden orb of light,
Which rules the day, and dissipates the night,—
That glittering diamond in our system's ring,—
Is it not *Sol* to which we owe the spring?
Our yearly revolutions round that globe,
In one sense, make the varying seasons robe,
Successively, our land in heat and cold,
And make it now look young, anon quite old;
But were the sun extinguished from the sky
Poor orphaned earth would totter, fall, and die.
Dependant on his aid for warmth and light,
And strong attraction to direct her right,
If he were gone eternal death and gloom
Would make our natal star our fatal tomb.
Though changing times would cease if earth should pause

The lamp of day is still the pristine cause ;
And should our world eternalize its run,
We look in vain for springs without the sun.
And as in Nature's changes so in grace,
The day-spring from on high but shows his face,
And life, and light, and liberty ensue,
For He it is who maketh all things new.
And when, delivered from the wintry state
Of sin, the soul its second birth can date ;
While passing to its gracious Lover's breast,
Where, nestling, 'twill enjoy the sweetest rest ;
As on immortal pinions it doth fly
To Him who bled that it might never die,
Though it must know no halt, but still pursue
The heavenly way, till Jesus come in view,—
Though without motion it would cease to live,
Yet that alone could ne'er existence give ;
Its life is in the Sun of Righteousness,
From whom proceeds each ray of happiness,
With many pure illuminating beams,
Through which the earth a heaven in embryo seems.
'Tis brightest day if He go forth in might ;
If He withdraw, 'tis black Egyptian night :
If He arise with healing in his wings,
The Christian's soul, and all within him sings.
Dull, sullen winter speedily is gone,
The garb of praise, for heaviness, is on ;

No longer on the willows hangs the harp
In silence mute; though Babylonians carp,
And though the land be strange, yet sing he will,
The love of Christ his happy heart doth fill:
Full well he knows that should he hold his peace,
The stones from crying out could never cease.
So, while the day-star is the fount of joy
Without, Jesus doth inwardly employ
The noblest powers of the Christian's soul,
As on he wends his way to glory's goal.
Sin's icy season now with Him is o'er;
His change is past, He'll change on earth no more:
No radical mutation will he know
Until His disembodied spirit go
To bathe in oceans of supreme delight,
And walk with ecstacy the fields of light:
Then darkness will be lost in endless day,
And one unclouded summer reign for aye.

If yon transplendent luminary bring
Such festive joys, its glories we must sing.
Hail! noble Sun, whose overpowering rays
Bedazzle my weak vision as I gaze:
Thy generosity displayed in spring
Constrains the lyre to strike its heartist string.
Thou ancient fountain of refulgence, Hail!
(Sound and resound the echo, hill and dale.)
When spotless Adam did the world behold

Fresh as it issued from the Maker's mould,
Thy beams unfolded to his ravished eye
Delights that waked his soul to melody.
Thou still did'st shine as from the ark stepped Noah;
Thy face was seen when Lot escaped to Zoar.
When Joshua encountered Israel's foe,
Thy majesty was not in haste to go;
The servant of the Lord but said, "Stand still,"
And promptly thou did'st heed thy Ruler's will.
Again, when Hezekiah sought a sign
That God would spare his life from swift decline,
Thou wert arrested, and full ten degrees,
Did'st backward turn, thy Source of light to please.
So, on that memorable day of gloom
When Jesus met the sinner's wrathful doom,
From Calvary's tragic spectacle, with awe
Thou did'st thy luminiferous aid withdraw.
And till the temple's vail was torn in twain,—
Till splitting rocks by bursting eased their pain,—
Till quaking earth a second life bestowed
On those who long had filled their last abode,—
Till Christ, our potent Champion, put to flight
The alien armies of the prince of night,—
Till round the concave "It is finished!" rung,
And each angelic voice the triumph sung,—
Till every enemy in chains was led,
And our Almighty Victor bowed his head,—

Till God was satisfied,—redemption wrought,—
And free salvation for believers bought,—
Till, not a fraction left for man to do,
All was complete,—in short, till Jesus knew
The plan of grace accomplished, and had died,—
Thou did'st not fail, O Sun! thy face to hide.
But when the purpose of eternity
Was carried out, and when the great decree,
That God's own Son should for the sinner die,
Was perfectly fulfilled, then from on high
Thy lustrous beams shot out again, to show
A ruined world the only Way from woe:
The one exclusive Ransom of the lost,
His life their pattern, and His death their cost.
And since that weightiest of events took place,
Thou hast not halted on thy splendent race.
Shine on, thou glittering ball of brightness! shine,
Emit His glory who first kindled thine;
Cease not thy dazzling flood abroad to pour,
Till Christ arrive thou'lt ne'er be darkened more.
But when He shall appear thou'lt flee away,
At His approach 'twere arrogance to stay;
For thou to Him art but the morning star,—
Forerunner of the day not distant far.
Our cry shall be, till all Thy splendours fail,—
Primeval source of pure refulgence, hail!

Listen! the feathery choir my Muse remind

That spring delights are more to earth confined
Than to the sun. I therefore would attend
Their call, and from my eagle flight descend.
But as I on a sunbeam sink, a lark,
Warbling with glee, is skyward soaring; hark!
How merrily he carols out his song,
Which as he rises sounds more sweet and strong.
On quivering pinions loftily he flies
To seek retreat in calm, untroubled skies:
And, like the summoned soul when heaven it nears,
He fades, he vanishes, he disappears.
Would that we all were larks, that, leaving earth,
Where real joy is drowned in sinful mirth,
We might upon the wings of faith and love,
Mount upward to our Father's home above
To sing the happy songs, unmixed with sighs,
Which warble from the birds of Paradise.
  To hear the rich exuberance of joy
Effused from gleesome birds, one must enjoy;
Nor do we envy that cold mass of clay,
Misnamed a man, that's never moved to pray
That he may laud his God but half so well
As morning lark, or evening Philomel;
Or friendly Robin, in his scarlet vest,
Applauding Him who tinged his florid breast.
The vocal jubilations of the grove
Arouse our sluggish hearts where'er we rove:

The whistling thrush, the little twittering wren,
The chirping sparrow, all become to men
Instructors in the sacred work of praise,
And teach Creation's lords the purest lays.
  Though we forget the God of providence,
And of his goodness feel so slight a sense,—
Though we are deaf to Nature's thankful voice,—
Though we are dumb when other tongues rejoice,—
Yet these, protected from the stormy blast,
Are full of gratefulness for mercies past:
Their songs proclaim the kindness of that Friend
Who shelters all that on His care depend.
When Jesus came to sojourn here below,
The punishment for sin to undergo,
Few *men* the mercy of His mission sung;—
The midnight sky with acclamation rung,
For angels came to tell the wondrous story;
From every lip burst forth the keynote, "Glory!"
Hark! the seraphic solo thrills the air,—
"Fear not! good tidings of great joy I bear;
"To-day is born a Saviour, Christ the Lord:"
Then suddenly, with rapture and accord,
Transported legions shout aloud "Amen;
Glory to God, goodwill and peace to men."
But while cherubic tongues this birthday keep,
Where is the sinner? He is sound asleep
Though justly doomed to everlasting pain,

And totally unable to obtain
Exemption,—yet when Jesus, full of love,
Quits His exalted throne of power above,
And clothes His Godhead with our sinful clay
That He may live and die to take away
The curse of sin, the bitter pangs of hell,
And lift the rebel up with Him to dwell
In immortality,—man fails to raise
One note of welcome, or one song of praise,
Though angels felt the loss of Jesus most,
Yet Hallelujahs filled the heavenly host;
And though to save our race He stooped to earth,
No human tongue was fired to hail His birth!
So still, while every bird prepares a lay,
Man fails his meed of gratitude to pay.
   Hush! 'tis the cuckoo's note salutes my ear,
In strain which every rambler stops to hear.
His undiversified, monotonous
Announcement of the spring, would bring to us
Greater delight, if there did but belong
More cadence and inflection to his song.
However, as his Maker made him so,
We'll not complain—let criticism go;
And as we're always glad to hear his voice,
We'll brook his sameness and with him rejoice.
   While animating birds engross our thought,
The unassuming flowers attention court.

And who does not with ardency admire
What we might term creation's floral choir?
For though they never chant His praise abroad,
Their charms proclaim the beauty of the Lord.
The unobtrusive snowdrop chastely bows
To welcome Spring, and pay its yearly vows:
The primrose pale, with faint and sickly smell,
Betrays its dwelling in the dankish dell,
And on the wayside ridge,—though that above,
Many, we for its early advent love:
The lowly daisy, either with a red
Or snowy crown upon its golden head,
Bestuds each bank, bespangles every lawn,
And with allurements doth the glen adorn:
The yellow buttercup, with glossy hue
O'erlays with beauty's gilt the vernal view:
The virgin lily of the vale likewise,
Imbosomed in its secret birthplace lies:
The cowslip, daffodil, anemone,
And hyacinth, enliven all we see;
While hosts of other flowers rise to view,
Speckling earth's emerald floor so fresh and new.
But in our musings let us not forget,
The diffident, yet odorous violet.
The essence of the Spring is here contained:
Well has it partiality obtained.
Its sweet attractions make a favourite

Of this perfumed and bashful floweret.
Why dost thou hide away thy drooping head?
Why keep so close within thy shady bed,
Endearing gem? We'd gladly have thee where
We always might inhale thy fragrant air.
How modestly thy purple head is bent;
How rich thy colour, and how sweet thy scent.
From thee, pet flower, we would learn to be
Examples of unfeigned humility.
  How glorious is the time of Spring! the whole
Of nature seems replete with joy. The soul
That can the scene behold, and have no song
To sing, or feel no rapture, must belong
To some contemptible, degraded class
Of beings viler than the brutes. Alas!
There are those who delight in nothing pure
Or good; nor can their grovelling minds endure
To ponder God's fair universe to find
His finger-prints of power and love combined
In each component part. While with the heart
By grace renewed, the studies that impart
Profoundest pleasure, are the Books divine—
Nature and Revelation,—both which shine
Like full-orbed suns across the Christian's road,
Lighting his steps to Glory's blest abode.
  The chord is touched! my bosom vibrates! Thought
Has to its happy home my spirit brought.

Imagination! fold thy fiery wing,
Awhile we'll wait; for here a brighter spring
Than e'er below inflamed a poet's soul,
Doth ceaselessly round God its centre roll.
We're now in heaven, at rest (sometimes we say
Would we we're really so!) here all is day,
Black night has here no seat; and nought but bliss
Finds an abode in such a world as this.
But list! The voice of my Beloved sounds!
His foot upon the hills and mountains bounds.
He shows himself,—he speaks,—what does he say?
"Rise up, my love, my fair one, come away.
"Lo! winter's past; sin's frigid blasts are o'er,
"The damps of persecution are no more:
"The icy fetters of the despot Death,
"Are broken by my Spirit's quickening breath:
"And carnal Self, the vilest foe of all,
"Has lost the field, and met his final fall.
"The rain is gone;—no longer clouds suspend
"Their fulness, coming showers to portend:
"Affliction's storms are spent; the latest drop
"Has fallen, and secured the promised crop
"Of blessedness unmingled with alloy,
"And all that sowed in tears have reaped in joy.
"The pelting torrents of the wrath of God,
"Are here unknown, and His chastising rod,
"With which on earth He brought His children home,

'Is now destroyed, for hence they'll never roam.
'The testing pangs of poverty are o'er,
'No want is heard of on this affluent shore;
'Though rich, for your sake I became as poor
'As you, to make you rich for evermore.
'The loveliest flowers on this earth appear;—
'(This new earth formed by Him who brought you here):
'All that was beauteous in the world of time,—
'Then in the bud—has now attained its prime;
'And, happy thought! this garden bears no trace
'Of direful guilt,—it never reached this place.
'The rose here flourishes without the thorn,
'No thistle by this weedless soil is borne.
'Divine perfection permeates this land,
'Untarnished by the touch of human hand.
'The season of the songs of birds is come;—
'Hark how my saints and angels sing! The hum
'Of earthly dissonance for ever hushed;
'For ever still the speechless groans that gushed
'From the pent soul aspiring to be free
'As denizen of immortality;
'Snapped are the shackles of imprisonment,
'By irreversible enfranchisement.
'Hark! hark! their shouts outswell the far-heard voice
'Of multitudes, or the still louder voice
'Of many rivers rushing down the fall,
'Or that with which the mighty thunders call.—

"Here in these outer courts no longer stay,
"Arise, my love, my fair one, come away."
Jesus! I come; to thy dear arms I fly,
That, like a helpless lamb, my soul may lie
In thy kind bosom; or, as tender John
Was wont to do on earth, recumb upon
The downy pillow of Thy loving breast
And there find undisturbed, eternal rest.
Thou wert the pearl of price for which I sought;
Thou wert the crown for which the fight I fought;
Thou of the dove—my spirit—wert the ark;
Thou wert the haven of my shattered bark;
Thou wert the prize for which I ran the race;
Thou wert the magnet which increased my pace,
When through the world I did a pilgrim roam,
England my lodge, Jerusalem my home.
I'd none that I desired on earth's lone ball
But Thee; and now in Thee I have my all.
Thanks, everlasting thanks to Thee, Thou dear,
Thou precious Friend! but for Thy love I here
Had never been: Thou did'st Thy Throne forsake
To save our race: Thou did'st a body take,
And all our sins and griefs were on Thee laid,
That, being like us then, we might be made
Like to Thee now. But here I mostly see
Thy wondrous grace, that Thou did'st die for *me*.
Oh this was grace indeed! its only fount

Those precious thoughts, which none can ever count.
And now that I am with Thee where Thou art,
With love reciprocal enlarge my heart,
Open my lips with song, and fire my lays,
Unloose my tongue to hymn Thy worthy praise:
And while I view the splendid Spring that reigns
Throughout these holy, happy, blest domains,—
While all around is joy,—help me to blend
My highest powers of music, and to spend
The long eternity that now with me
Begins, in blessing and adoring Thee.
Hence let my Hallelujah swell the strain,
"Jehovah God Omnipotent doth reign."

" MY CANDLE WILL SOON BE OUT. "

The hour was late, and the night was dark,
The blast was severely keen,
While, wrapped in gloom, in a dismal room,
A woman at work was seen.
And as she plied her needle, she eyed
Her glimmer with anxious doubt;
And, faint and sick, said, " I must be quick,
My candle will soon be out."

O man of God! by the burial clod,
Which soon may be turned for thee;
By life's brief stay, by the judgment day,
By time, by eternity.
With every nerve thy Redeemer serve,
And spend not a day without
Striving to win precious souls from sin,
For thy candle will soon be out.

Thy Master's course, till he reached the cross,
  Was one of incessant toil:
He bore thy woes, He subdued thy foes,
  That thou mightest share the spoil.
To do God's will, His law to fulfil,
  He constantly went about;
With every power, He improved each hour,
  As His candle would soon be out.

Be stirred, my soul, thou art near thy goal,
  Time flies on the swiftest wing;
Work while 'tis day, and in every way
  Thy powers into action bring.
Let my life be bright as a shining light,
  My spirit like Christ's, devout;
My days are few, there is much to do,
  My candle will soon be out.

O Sinner! think of the feeble link
  Which holds thee above the grave;
If that should snap—oh woeful mishap—
  No power thy soul could save.
Hell is the end to which sinners tend,
  And short is the longest route;
Weigh well thy fate, ere it be too late,
  Thy candle will soon be out.

Whate'er you be you will shortly see
 The Judge of the earth appear,
Now—*now* be wise, for the dread assize,
 The day of the Lord is near.
To fix your fate in a changeless state,
 The Lord will descend with a shout;
O seek his face in this day of grace,
 For your candle will soon be out.

"REJOICE IN THE LORD."

REJOICE in the Lord, poor sin-bitten soul!
As Moses uplifted the serpent-crowned pole,
So Christ is exalted on high to impart
The balm of salvation and health to thy heart.

Rejoice in the Lord, disconsolate saint!
Like David cast down, like Gideon faint;
Repose on the arm which constructed the world,
And mountains of grief shall to ruin be hurled.

The sinner may quake when trouble is near,
But what has the child of Jehovah to fear?
The voice which commanded the starlights to shine,
In tenderest accents exclaims, "I am thine!"

Rejoice in the Lord, defender of truth,
In the snow of thy age, or the dew of thy youth;
Thy work may be heavy, yet be not cast down,
The labour is brief, but eternal the crown.

O Christian! O Christian! how canst thou be sad?
Away with thy griefs, rejoice and be glad:
The world's airy bubble no joy can afford,
For strong consolation rejoice in the Lord.

Rejoice in the Lord, and never give way
To terror by night, nor sorrow by day;
The white-crested billows on life's heaving seas,
But hasten thy rest in the harbour of ease.